Cadillac Press
185 Drummond St. Rd
Drummond, NB E3Y 1V9
Canada

2 4 6 8 10 9 7 5 3 1

FIRST EDITION

Boo and Oscar

For Amelia
&
Ryker

in
Hot Air Heroics

Wendy L. Koenig

by Wendy L. Koenig   **Illustrations by Shelbie Donald**
Cadillac Press

Boo the cat and Oscar the spider were walking through the countryside on a hot September morning. Boo said, "Today's a grand day for a big adventure."

"What shall we do?"

"I don't know. I can't think of anything."

Suddenly, a giant shadow passed over them.

"Was that a bird? It might eat me!" Oscar hid in Boo's fur and trembled with fear.

Boo looked up at a giant hot-air balloon above them. He pointed. "Look!"

The people in the balloon's basket waved. Then he looked around and saw other balloons. "Where are they coming from?"

"Over there." Oscar pointed again, this time at a big yellow and black balloon that looked like a giant bumble bee. It was climbing into the sky, and it didn't seem to be too far away.

Boo ran to the nearby field, Oscar bouncing on his back. There were so many balloons, it looked like a field of giant, bright lollipops. Some of the balloons were ready to launch, and some were still stretched out flat on the ground. People were everywhere.

Oscar scrambled down from Boo's back and ran from balloon to balloon. "They're all so pretty!"

Boo was just about to agree when, right in front of him, a mouse scampered between people's feet, across the field, to a not-so-near balloon. Cats have very good eyes.

There were two mice, in fact! Boo's tail twitched. He loved mice.

They were playing and didn't see Boo sneak toward them. Then one looked up, saw the danger coming, squeaked loudly, and they both ran into the basket of the balloon.

Boo raced in after them, only to see them disappear through a tiny hole in the corner. He peered through the hole to see where they'd gone, but didn't spot a single whisker.

Through the sound of the people's shouts, the roar of the burners, and the tromp of feet, he heard Oscar calling him. "Boo! Where are you?"

Cats have very good ears, too.

Boo sat up and looked over the side. He started to answer, but just then, the basket lurched and swayed. Fresh air gusted through the mouse hole. Two little mice were waving to him. One stuck out its tongue. They held up the ends of chewed through ropes and laughed. Oscar was getting smaller and the clouds were getting bigger. The balloon was floating away!

"I'll save you!" Oscar's voice was very tiny and very far away. Boo could barely hear him, and cats have good ears.

Boo was really scared. He didn't know how to fly a balloon. He couldn't even reach the blower to turn it off and on. What if he crashed into something? What if he hit a power line?

Oscar ran to a balloon that was getting ready to launch. In a high, squeaky, spider voice, he said, "Follow that balloon!"

They set off in pursuit and it wasn't long before they caught up. Oscar climbed up the side of his balloon, attached a string of spider silk and swung over to Boo. He said, "I'll make a web you can walk across."

"A web won't hold me." He looked down to the ground. It was far away.

"I'll make it strong."

Oscar pulled out a book, "Web-making For Dummies", and started reading. After just a couple minutes, he shut the book with a 'snap' and an 'Aha!', and went back to work on his web.

First, he stretched ten or twelve long spider silk lines between the baskets of the two balloons. Then he wrapped another silk string around them. Around and around and around. And then around again. Back and forth. Back and forth. It took a long time.

Finally, it was ready.

Boo looked at the spider silk rope stretched across open air, then he looked at the ground. It was very, VERY far away. "I can't walk across that!"

Oscar squeaked, "You can. Just like a tightrope walker." He handed a pole to Boo.

With a gulp and a deep breath, Boo put one paw on the rope. It held. He put a second paw on the rope and it held, too. He stood up, holding the pole for balance, and began to inch across the spider silk tightrope to the other balloon.

Halfway there, he looked down.

The ground was very, VERY, VERY far away.

He closed his eyes and took another deep breath.

Oscar said, "You can do it."

Boo opened his eyes and slid his foot down the line.

Then the other. One step, two. One step, two.

One step.

Two.

Then he was across and Oscar helped him into the basket

of the rescue balloon.

"I'm glad you had that book," Boo said to Oscar.

"Me too. When we get down, I'm going to buy you a little red balloon and tie it to your tail so I don't lose you again."

Boo shook his head. "I think I've had enough of balloons for today." He smiled at Oscar.

Oscar smiled at him.

The sun was shining and the sky was blue. Boo said, "Well, maybe one more balloon ride."

It was a good day for a grand adventure. And what an adventure that had been.

Manufactured by Amazon.ca
Bolton, ON